Contents

The Historian's Sources 2
    Documents 2
    Archaeology 2

The Anglo-Saxon and Viking Invasions 3

Why the Anglo-Saxons and Vikings came to Britain 5
    The Britons' need for protection 5
    The need for new homes 6

Conquest by the Anglo-Saxons 8

Conquest by the Vikings 10
    Place Names 12

Ships and Sailors 13

Warriors and Weapons 17

Defence of the Kingdoms 22

Houses 24

Farming and Village Life 26

The Lord and the Hall 31

The Lord's Lady 33

Kin, Law and Government 34
    Wergild 34
    The duties of the family 35
    Trials 35
    Trial by ordeal 35
    Punishments 36

Town Life 37

Religion 41
    Christianity 42
    Unification of the Church 43
    The Vikings and the Christians 44
    The Church and learning 45
    Church buildings 46

The Anglo-Saxon Period and Us 48

The Historian's Sources

If we want to find out where a river begins we can travel along its length to its origin or source. If a historian wishes to find out about an event in the past or how people lived, unfortunately he cannot get into a time machine and travel back. Instead he must study the objects and documents people have left behind. Historians call the objects and documents they use their 'sources'. They are the historian's evidence.

Documents

These are very important sources for the historian. They can tell him not only what people did, but why they did something. However, many documents have been lost or destroyed and even those which remain are not always easy to use.

The documents used in this book were originally written in Latin or Anglo-Saxon, as in this illustration. For your use they have been translated into modern English.

Have you ever heard about a football match from a player on each of the opposing teams? Each player may have only told you about hs side's good points and the other side's faults. Sometimes the writers used by historians have done the same sort of thing. We say that such a writer was biased – that he or she wrote a one-sided account.

Another difficulty may be that what somebody wrote down was not exactly what happened. Perhaps you have played the game of Chinese Whispers and laughed at how the sentence changed as it passed around the group. When the Saxons first came to Britain they did not read and write and so their first history was written down many years later. We cannot always be sure how much of this history is true.

Archaeology

The objects people have left behind – tools, buildings, pots, clothing – are called archaeological sources.

How many of the objects which we use today will survive to be studied by archaeologists in the future?

Coins are fairly easy to date and often provide an important clue to the age of articles found with them. These gold coins were found buried with a ship at Sutton Hoo, Suffolk.

The Anglo-Saxons and Vikings usually built with wood which rots away. However, the holes left in the ground, like these found at Chalton, Hampshire, tell us something about the buildings which once stood there.

The Anglo-Saxon and Viking Invasions

At the beginning of the fifth century, nearly 1600 years ago, the Romans left Britain. The **Anglo-Saxon Chronicle,** a diary of events written by monks between AD 800 and AD 1160 tells us:

1. AD 409: In this year Rome was attacked by the Goths. After this year the Romans no longer ruled Britain. They had ruled there 470 years, since Julius Caesar first came to the country.
    AD 418: In this year the Romans collected all the treasures which were in Britain and hid some in the earth so that noone afterwards could find them and some they took with them into Gaul.

A little later the **Anglo-Saxon Chronicle** gives us more details.
2. AD 443: In this year the Britons sent across the sea to Rome for help against tribes which were attacking them, but they got no help from the Romans because their troops were waging war against Attila the Hun.

During the six centuries which followed the break-up of the Roman Empire many tribes invaded and settled in different parts of Europe. The first group of tribes which conquered the area now known as England – meaning 'Land of the Angles' – are generally called the Anglo-Saxons. They mainly consisted of Jutes, Angles, Saxons and Frisians. The later tribes who spread across Europe, attacking, conquering and settling, are usually known as the Vikings or Danes. Like the Anglo-Saxons, they were made up of different peoples: Norse, Danes and Swedes.

3

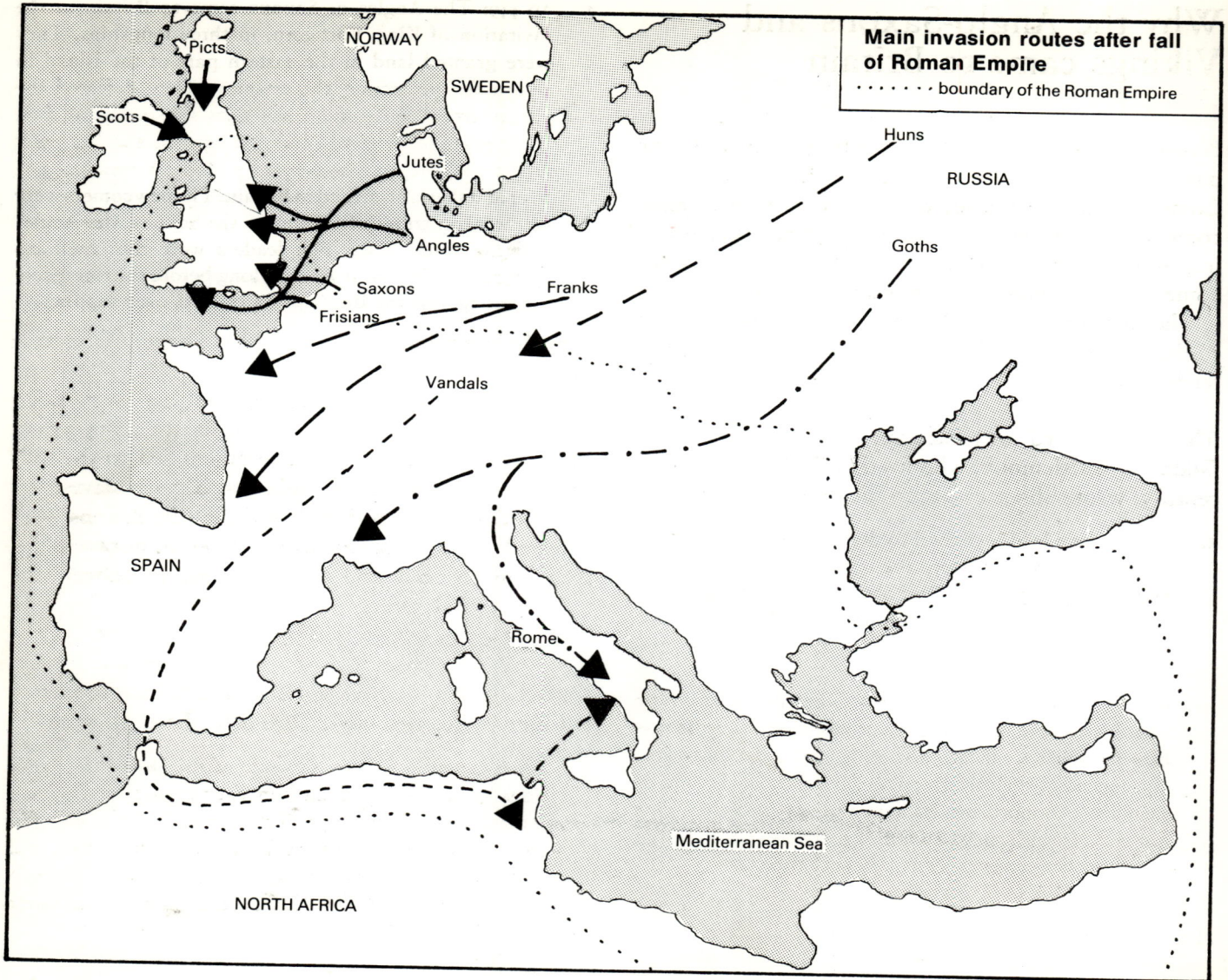

Main invasion routes after fall of Roman Empire

· · · · · · · boundary of the Roman Empire

NORWAY

SWEDEN

Picts

Scots

Jutes

Angles

Saxons

Franks

Frisians

Huns

RUSSIA

Goths

Vandals

SPAIN

Rome

NORTH AFRICA

Mediterranean Sea

Why the Anglo-Saxons and Vikings came to Britain

People living in Britain today come from many different parts of the world. Some have come from Commonwealth countries to find work. Others have come to escape from governments which have killed and imprisoned people of their race or religion. Others have come to join friends and families already here.

The Anglo-Saxons and Vikings were also immigrants to this country. Why did they leave their homelands to settle here?

The Britons' need for protection

Gildas, a British monk, who lived in Wales in the sixth century, wrote about events in the previous century.

3. The Britons held a council to decide what was the best and safest way to stop the frequent invasions and plunderings of the Picts and Scots. The members of the assembly along with their proud tyrant leader did not think carefully enough of the future. The protection they chose for their country was in fact its destruction. They invited the wild Saxons, hated by God and men, into the island to defend it against the northern invaders. It was like inviting a wolf into a sheepfold. The Saxons came and settled in the eastern part of the island. Hearing of their success, more Saxons joined them. Soon they were not content with their reward of monthly supplies from the Britons and they rebelled against them.

Bede, an Anglo-Saxon monk, wrote the following in about AD 731.

4. AD 449: The Angles or Saxons came to Britain at the invitation of King Vortigern, in three longships. They were granted land in the eastern part of the island in return for protecting the country. They defeated the enemy from the north. They then sent news to their homelands of their success, adding that the land was fertile and the Britons cowardly. More warriors came over and they also settled in Britain. The newcomers were of the main tribes of Germany: the Saxons, the Angles and the Jutes. Their first leaders were the chieftains Hengist and Horsa. It was not long before the foreigners turned against the Britons in a quarrel over supplies.

Why do you think Bede's account is different from that of Gildas?

Gildas and Bede described how the battles between the invaders and the Britons went on for many years. Many Britons were killed. The others fled to the hills and forests. Some were caught and became slaves.

Both Gildas and Bede believed that the Britons were defeated as a punishment sent by God for not worshipping him properly and for not trying to convert the Saxons into Christians.

Other monks writing much later, after the Anglo-Saxons had become Christians, also believed raiders were being sent to Britain by God. The following extract is from the Peterborough Chronicle about AD 870.

5. Then came the Danes, servants of the Devil. Like mad dogs and robbers coming from their dens, they suddenly landed from their ships. They burned cities, villages, monasteries and slaughtered old men, young men and children. God sometimes makes his people suffer to see if their faith is strong and other times he makes them suffer to punish them.

Today historians usually look for several different reasons to explain why and when something happened.

Not just written evidence, but archaeology gives us some clues about the date of the Anglo-Saxons' arrival in Britain. Knowing this date is important because it helps us in the search for reasons behind their arrival.

The Saxons are believed to have come from north Germany. Graves have been found there, containing shields, spears and swords. Similar graves have been found in England dating from the fifth century onwards. Possibly these belonged to the tribes who were asked by Hengist and Horsa to send more troops.

The Angles and Jutes may have come from further north in Germany. There pots containing burial ashes have been found. Such pots have been found all over England dating from the fifth century onwards. Many of the pots are very similar and some archaeologists believe they could even have been made by the same potter. It is unlikely that these pots were used by the Britons who, as Christians, did not cremate their dead.

The need for new homes

In northern Europe many more graves have been found dating from the years AD 400 to 600 than from previous years. Historians regard this as evidence that the population was increasing and that there were therefore more people to feed than before.

The tribes who lived in the Anglo-Saxon homelands did not read or write. However, we can learn something about their land from **Tacitus,** a Roman, who wrote about the tribes living between the river Elbe and the river Ems in AD 98.

6. Dark woods and sodden marshland. The marshy ground was perilous to strangers. One could only proceed on a narrow road built through a vast swamp. All around was slimy, treacherous bog, clinging mud crossed by streams, beyond which were thick forests. The land was continuously clad in fog.

From the Laxdaela Saga we get a clue as to why the Vikings settled in Britain.

7. Ketil Flatnose preferred to go across the sea to Scotland because the living was good there. He knew the country well for he had raided there many times.

Pot found at Caistor, Norfolk.

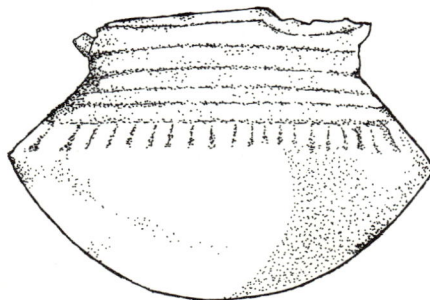

Pot found in Angeln, Denmark.

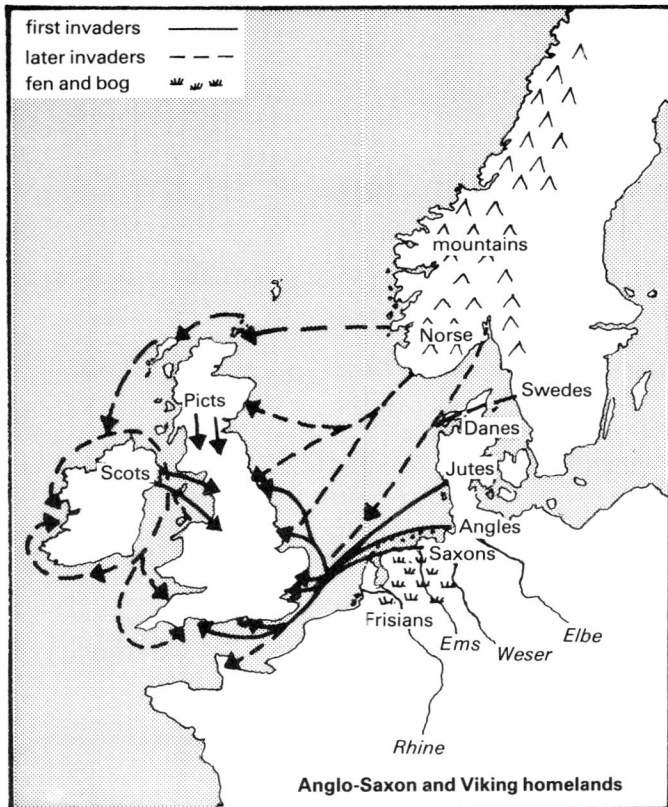

Anglo-Saxon and Viking homelands

Why might the Saxons and Vikings have come to Britain for land? Does Bede suggest that the Saxons came for this purpose? Using the documents and illustrations in this chapter to help you, can you suggest other reasons which the invaders may have had?

This treasure was found buried, probably for safe-keeping, on St. Ninian's Isle, Shetland. Treasures like this, often made up of gold and silver, attracted Viking raiders.

The word 'Viking' may come from an Old English word 'wic' meaning camp. So Viking could mean 'people from the camp'. However, some people believe that it comes from the Old Norse (Norwegian) word 'vik' meaning fjord or inlet. If you look at the map above you will see why the Vikings could be called 'people of the fjords'.

Conquest by the Anglo-Saxons

The following extracts were written by the monk **Gildas** when he was describing the invasion of Britain in the fifth century.

8. The Barbarians drive us into the sea, the sea drives us back to the Barbarians; and between one and the other we are either slain or drowned.

   The heathens destroyed all the neighbouring cities and lands ... burned nearly the whole surface of the island from the eastern shore to the western shore. Many Britons were massacred, some surrendering for food were instantly killed, others stayed in Britain but not without fear, hiding in the hills, dense forests and rocks of the sea.

Gildas was a Christian and a Briton so perhaps we cannot expect him to write a good report about the heathens who were conquering his land. So before we accept his account of events, we must look at more evidence.

Bede wrote the following about events in the year AD 493.

9. The Britons slowly began to take heart and recover their strength coming out of hiding. They prayed to God that he would save them from being completely wiped out. Their leader at this time was Ambrosius Aurelianus. Under his leadership the Britons took up arms, challenged their conquerors to battle, and with God's help defeated them. There were several battles, sometimes one side won, sometimes the other, until the Battle of Badon Hill, when the Britons defeated the invaders, killing a great many of them. This took place about 44 years after the invaders had arrived in Britain.

A very old Welsh Chronicle written about the time of the invasions, says

10. AD 516/8 the Battle of Badon in which Arthur carried the cross of Jesus Christ for three days and nights on his shoulders, and the Britons were victorious.

The leader of the Britons 'Ambrosius Aurelianus' mentioned by Bede and the Arthur mentioned in the Welsh Chronicle are probably the same man. Perhaps this Arthur is the King Arthur of legend. Other chroniclers wrote a lot more about him and many stories grew up around his name. Unfortunately we do not know where Mount Badon is, nor most of the other places mentioned in these documents.

From objects such as pots found in Anglo-Saxon cemeteries, archaeologists believe the Anglo-Saxons first settled along the east and south-eastern coasts of Britain and gradually spread westwards.

It is thought that the Anglo-Saxons travelled inland by using the rivers. Their shallow-bottomed boats would have been very suitable for this. There are many rivers along the east coast of Britain which they could have used.

By AD 700 the invaders had driven the ruling Britons out of most of their old homelands. The Britons and Welsh only controlled what is now Wales and Devon and Cornwall. The Scots and Picts had been driven northwards and the Anglo-Saxon part of Britain soon began to be known as England.

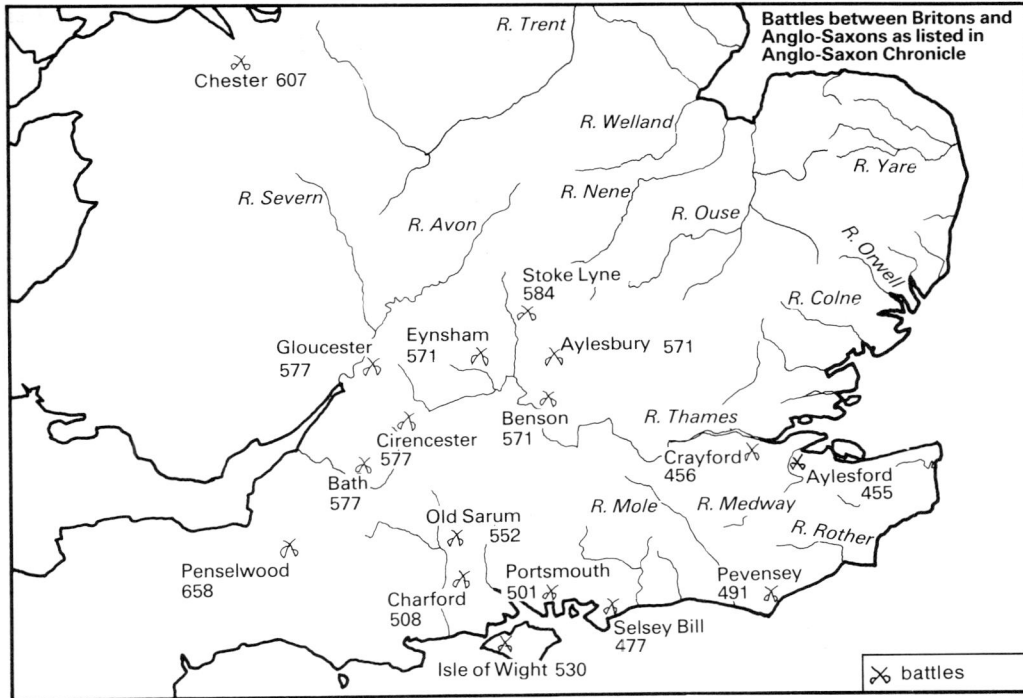

Battles between Britons and Anglo-Saxons as listed in Anglo-Saxon Chronicle

Chester 607

R. Trent

R. Welland

R. Yare

R. Severn

R. Nene

R. Ouse

R. Orwell

R. Avon

R. Colne

Stoke Lyne 584

Gloucester 577

Eynsham 571

Aylesbury 571

Benson 571

R. Thames

Cirencester 577

Crayford 456

Aylesford 455

Bath 577

R. Mole

R. Medway

Old Sarum 552

R. Rother

Penselwood 658

Portsmouth 501

Pevensey 491

Charford 508

Selsey Bill 477

Isle of Wight 530

✂ battles

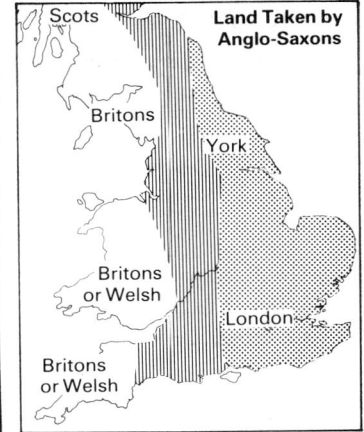

Land Taken by Anglo-Saxons

Scots

Britons

York

Britons or Welsh

London

Britons or Welsh

Key

▨ Anglo-Saxons 5th Century

▥ Anglo-Saxons 7th Century

☐ Britons

Battles between Britons and Anglo-Saxons as listed in the **Anglo-Saxon Chronicle.**

Some other battles cannot be shown because we do not know where they took place. How many years were there between the first and last battles? Did the Anglo-Saxons conquer Britain quickly? Were the earliest battles in the east or west?

Compare this map with the map showing the land taken by the Anglo-Saxons. Do they agree? Did the first battles take place in the part of Britain archaeologists think was settled first? How does this evidence compare with what Gildas wrote (item 6).

Badbury Rings, Iron Age hillfort, Dorset: possibly Badon Hill. ▶

9

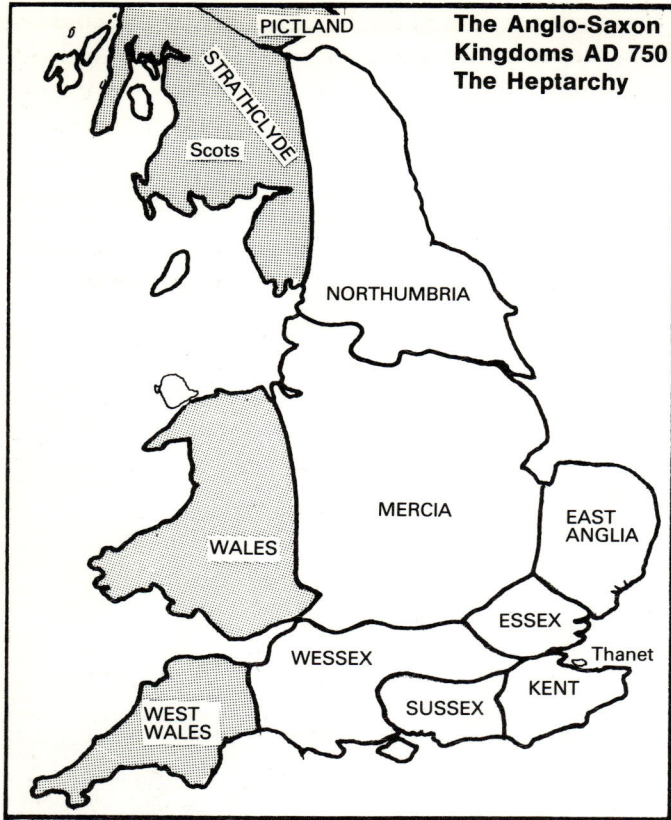

The Anglo-Saxon kingdoms AD 750 – the Heptarchy (from a Greek word meaning rule of seven).

Conquest by the Vikings

By AD 750 England was divided into the seven Anglo-Saxon kingdoms. To the north were the kingdoms of the Scots and Picts and to the west were the Welsh and West Welsh. Many of the kings who ruled these kingdoms had become Christians but they still fought each other for land and power. The **Anglo-Saxon Chronicle** tells us:

11. AD 752 In this year Cuthred King of Wessex fought against Aethelbald, King of Mercia, and put him to flight. AD 755. In this year Cynewulf took King Sigeberht's kingdom away from him. Sigeberht's brother killed Cynewulf. Aethelbald, King of Mercia, was murdered at Repton. Offa seized the kingdom of Mercia after he had fought Aethelbald's successor, Beornred, who was a bad ruler.

Another threat to the safety of the Anglo-Saxons came from the sea. This was attack by the Vikings, or Danes as they are often called in the chronicles and sagas. The **Anglo-Saxon Chronicle** states that:

12. AD 793 In this year great flashes of lightning and fiery dragons were seen flying through the air. These bad omens frightened the people of Northumbria. A great famine followed these signs. A little later the heathens came and destroyed God's Church in Lindisfarne and slaughtered the people.

The different tribes which made up the Anglo-Saxons did not live peacefully together. For many years they fought for control of the land not only against the Britons but also against each other. By AD 750 England was divided into three big and powerful kingdoms – Northumbria, Mercia, Wessex – and four smaller ones.

Unlike the Anglo-Saxons who had come to Britain in groups of two or three boats, the Vikings came in much larger numbers. Often between 20 and 30 ships would be together, but sometimes there would be as many as 350. No wonder the people were frightened.

Many years after AD 793 the **Anglo-Saxon Chronicle** tells us of Viking attacks. At first the Vikings did not stay. They raided the countryside, robbed the monasteries of their precious jewels and gold and silver and then returned to their homelands for the winter.

For the year AD 855, however, the **Anglo-Saxon Chronicle** tells us:

13. In this year for the first time the heathen stayed for the winter in Sheppey.

For 30 years the English kings fought hard to stop the Vikings or Danes invading, but in AD 886 Alfred of Wessex, the strongest English king, decided it would be better to make an agreement with the Danes to divide England between them. The boundary between the two parts went along the Roman road, Watling Street.

The English kingdoms and Danelaw AD 886.

Which kingdoms became Danelaw? Why do you think Danelaw was on the eastern side of Britain?

Anglo-Saxon treasure.

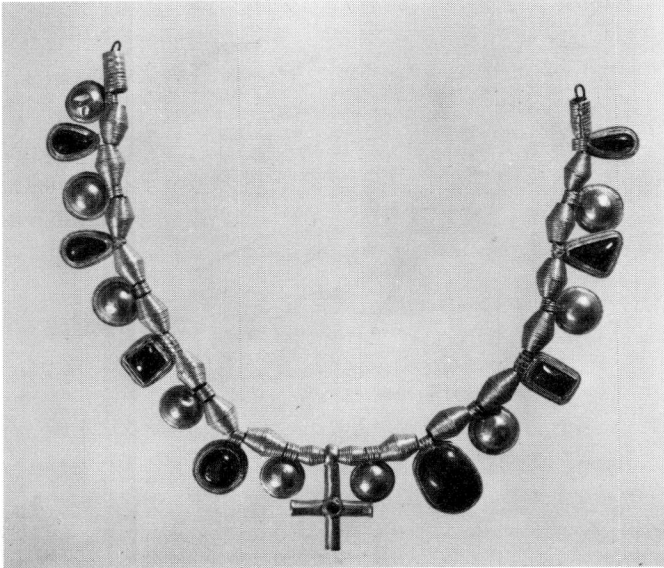

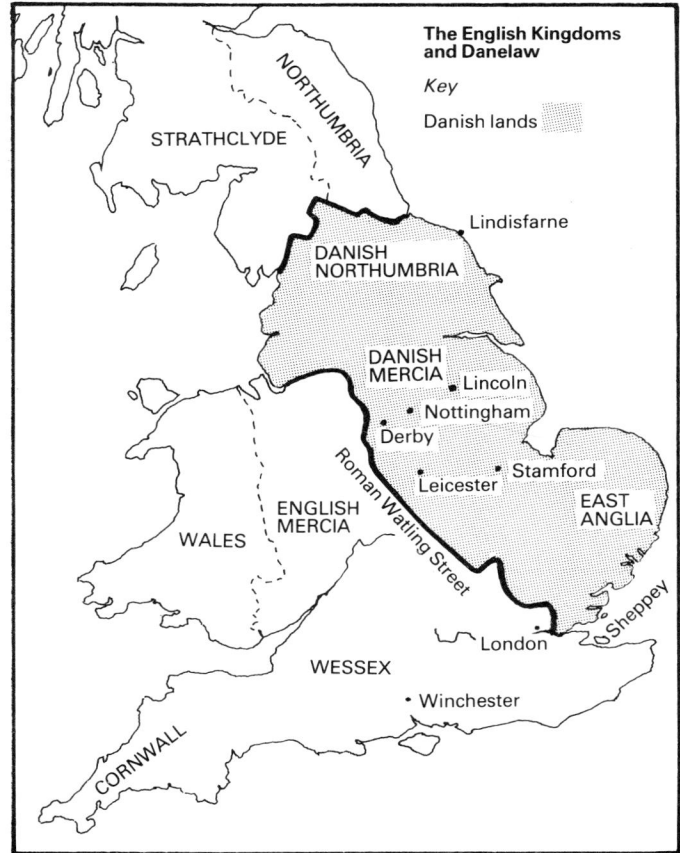

The English Kingdoms and Danelaw

Key

Danish lands

STRATHCLYDE
NORTHUMBRIA
Lindisfarne
DANISH NORTHUMBRIA
DANISH MERCIA
Lincoln
Nottingham
Derby
Leicester
Stamford
EAST ANGLIA
ENGLISH MERCIA
WALES
Roman Watling Street
Sheppey
London
WESSEX
Winchester
CORNWALL

Place Names

Place names help historians to know where the different groups of invaders settled. Here are some of the most common.

Modern ending	Anglo-Saxon meaning
ing	the people of . . . Reading in Berkshire was the place of the people of Reada, their leader
ham	homestead or small settlement
ton	farm or village
ford	shallow river crossing
den or dene	place in the woods for feeding pigs or valley
lea, ly, leigh	a clearing in the woods
bury, burgh	a fortified place or town
minster	monastery or church
wick, wich	farmstead or small village
worth	land with a hedge or fence round it, an enclosure

Modern ending	Viking meaning
by	village or farmstead
thorpe	village or farmstead
kirk	church
toft	homestead
beck	small stream
gate	street or path
thwaite	field

ey and a endings are also usually Viking

Some settlements built in the Anglo-Saxon period have now disappeared, but their names can be found in present-day farm names or in old documents. Often aerial photographs will show where these deserted villages used to be. Can you see the outlines of buildings and paths on this photograph?

The Vikings did not drive the Anglo-Saxons away from their settlements but usually set up their own villages, often quite nearby. Look at a map of your home area and see if there are any place names of Anglo-Saxon or Viking origin.

By the time of the Norman Conquest in the 11th century, there were hundreds of Anglo-Saxon and Viking settlements all over England. Most towns and villages in existence today are on the sites of Anglo-Saxon or Viking settlements.

Ships and Sailors

As we have already seen, the Anglo-Saxons and Vikings had many possible reasons for coming to Britain. One was the need for more land to grow food.

Many people or tribes have needed more land or a better food supply, but they have been unable to get it. In this chapter we are going to look at one of the reasons for the success of the Anglo-Saxons and Vikings: their ships.

The Roman, **Tacitus,** described in about AD 90 the 'powerful fleets' of the tribes living in northern Germany.

14. The style of their ships differs from ours in this respect, there is a prow at each end with a beak ready to be driven forward. They do not have sails nor rows of oars, but the oars are free so they can row in either direction.

This is the reconstruction of a ship, dated AD 400, found at Nydam, South Jutland, Denmark. Do you think it is like the ship Tacitus wrote about in AD 90?

This is a modern artist's impression of a Roman ship. How does this ship differ from the Nydam ship?

Archaeologists at work on the Sutton Hoo excavations. Can you see the shape of the ship?

No early Anglo-Saxon ships have been found in Britain, but in 1939 archaeologists excavating a burial mound at Sutton Hoo in Suffolk came across the remains of a Saxon ship built between AD 600 and AD 650. The overlapping planks of wood of which the ship had been built were completely rotted away, leaving just their impression in the soil. Some of the iron nails which held the planks together remained in place. The ship was a huge open rowing boat with 40 oars. No mast was found but sails may have been fitted when the wind was in the right direction.

Other discoveries have shown the ways in which ships changed over the years. A ship discovered at Gokstad, Norway, dating from about AD 850, had 32 oars, 16 on each side. The oars, which were probably only used near the coast or when there was no wind, slotted through holes in the side of the ship. These holes could be closed with wooden shutters. The ship's mast was 12 m tall and its sail (11 m wide) was made of white woollen material with red sewn-on stripes. Like the Sutton Hoo ship it had over-lapping planks of wood. Tar was used to seal between the planks. It was steered by a large oar fitted to the back of one side – the steering side, or starboard. 64 shields were found on the Gokstad ship, but it could carry nearly 300 armed men.

Diagram of Sutton Hoo burial ship.

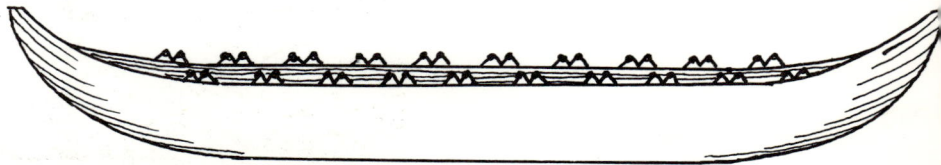

Wooden prow figure
from about AD 400.

The interior of a reconstructed ship, dated AD 850–900, found at Gokstad, Norway.

It was probably in ships like the Gokstad ship that the Vikings came to Britain. Here are some of the attacks listed in the **Anglo-Saxon Chronicle**.

15. AD 840: In this year Ealdorman Wulfheard fought against the crews of 33 ships and made a great slaughter.

    AD 841: In this year many men were killed by the heathen in Romney Marsh and later in the same year many men in Lindsey, East Anglia and Kent were killed by the enemy.

    AD 842: King Ethelwulf fought against the crews of 35 ships at Carhampton and the Danes won.

    AD 845: The people of Dorset and Somerset fought against the Danes at the mouth of the River Parret and won.

    AD 851: 350 ships came into the mouth of the Thames and stormed Canterbury and London.

The Viking ships were capable of sailing great distances. In several of the sagas there are stories of Vikings sailing to America. In 1892 a replica of the Gokstad ship sailed from Norway to America to prove it was possible. And, a few years ago, archaeologists discovered a Viking settlement in Newfoundland, an island off the coast of America. On page 40 you can see a map showing the Viking voyages and trade routes.

Some of the ships in the **Bayeux Tapestry**, which was embroidered in England shortly after the Norman invasion. The tapestry tells the story of the conquest of England by the Normans, descendants of the Vikings. Do you think the ships are like any of those which have been excavated?

Warriors and Weapons

The Roman, **Tacitus,** described the north German tribes:

16. They were big men who fought with long lances or spears. Their highest honour was to be thought of as a good warrior. These men were given the best places beside their chief and were given many gifts. Not to be a good warrior is a serious offence. Traitors and deserters are hung from trees; cowards and poor fighters are drowned in the marshes. As soon as a boy is considered old enough he is given a spear and shield by his family. Afterwards he will train with the older men for many years and hope to win fame in war. . . .

The chief is always a good fighter and all the other warriors try to be as good as he is. If the chief gets killed in battle it is a great disgrace for his warriors as it means they were not protecting him properly. It is also a disgrace to be defeated in battle. They fight until they have won or until there are no warriors left alive to defend their honour. The chief fights for victory, the followers for their chief.

The Battle of Maldon, a poem originally written in Old English, describes the battle between the English and the Vikings in AD 991. Here is part of it.

17. Byrhtnoth, the Lord of the English
ordered every warrior to dismount,
drive his horse away from the field,
and rely on his own skill and bravery.
Then he drew up his men,
told them how they should stand and keep their ranks,
and how best to hold their shields firm.

A Viking stood on the river bank opposite
and aggressively shouted:
'It would be better for you to buy off our raid with gold,
than that we, known for our cruelty,
should cut you down in battle.'
Byrhtnoth shouted this reply:
'We will pay you in whistling spears,
deadly darts and proven swords.
Weapons to pay you, pierce, split and slay you in storming battle.
We'll defend this land to the last ditch.
It would be much to our shame if you took our gold without battle.
No, you'll not get our treasure so easily.'
The Vikings waded the river Blackwater.
Their shields held high. . . .
Byrhtnoth ordered his men to form a wall with their shields
and to stand firm against the foe.
The time had now come for those who were doomed to die.
Spears and javelins flew from the hand . . .
Bows were busy, the rush of the battle was fierce,
Warriors fell on all sides, the young men lay dead. . . .
A Viking threw a spear which wounded Byrhtnoth.
This made him angry and with his spear he struck the proud Viking who had given him his wound,
He ran the spear through the young warrior's neck, killing him.
Then he hurled another spear at a raider,
splitting the Viking's plate chainmail,
the deadly spear piercing his heart.
But one of the seafarers sent a javelin
that struck Byrhtnoth. A young warrior standing by his side

quickly pulled it from Byrhtnoth's side
and hurled it back as hard as he could
at the man who had so badly injured his Lord.
The sharp point struck home, the Viking sagged and
    sank into the dust.
Another Viking, hoping to make short work
Of the injured Byrhtnoth and steal his jewels and
    sword, came near.
Byrhtnoth drew out his sword, but the enemy
    stopped him all too soon,
The golden hilted sword dropped from his hand.
He could no longer hold a weapon of any kind.
Supported by two faithful men,
he called to his men to continue the battle
and then he prayed to God. . . .
The Vikings struck him down, and the two men who
    were with him.
Both gave their lives in defence of their lord.
Then an ordinary soldier called out
'Who intends to avenge our lord's death?'
They hurried forward, not worrying about their own
    lives,
hoping to get revenge for the death of their chief. . . .

The end of this poem has been lost, but soon after the battle the English paid the Danes £20,000 to try to stop further attacks. This was called the Danegeld. It did not stop further attacks and soon Danegeld was a regular tax which the English had to pay.

From the description of the Battle of Maldon, you will see that, despite Byrhtnoth's organization of a wall of shields at the beginning of the fight, battles were not very organized affairs. Most of the fighting was hand to hand, using the spear for stabbing and the sword for slashing.

As Tacitus had written more than 800 years before, it was still thought to be shameful to leave the battlefield alive, or at least uninjured. You fought for your lord, and if he was killed you avenged his death.

From the descriptions of the battle in the poem you can see how the different weapons were used and also how important the shield was for defence.

The spear was the most common Anglo-Saxon or Viking weapon. It was used in hunting and war. Notice the 'wings' on spearhead 3. This is an improvement on early spearheads. The wings stopped the spear from going too far into a body and meant that it could be removed more easily. Spearheads varied in length from a few centimetres to nearly 50 cms.

▼

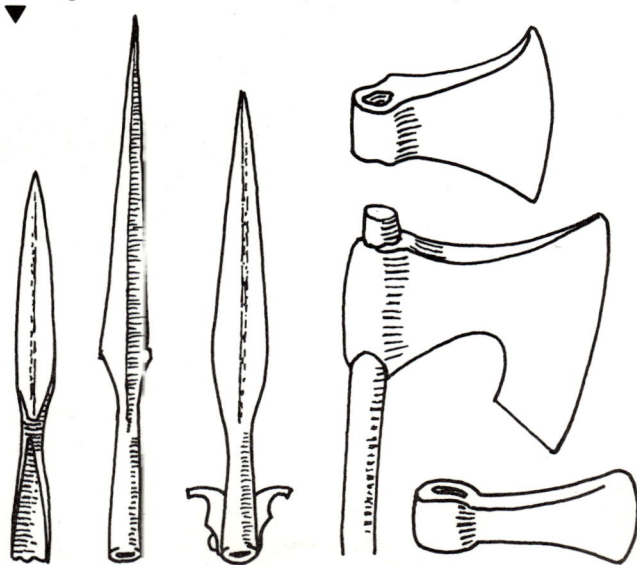

▲

Both Anglo-Saxons and Vikings used axes. After spears, they were probably the most common weapon. They were mainly used for hand-to-hand fighting, but also occasionally for throwing.

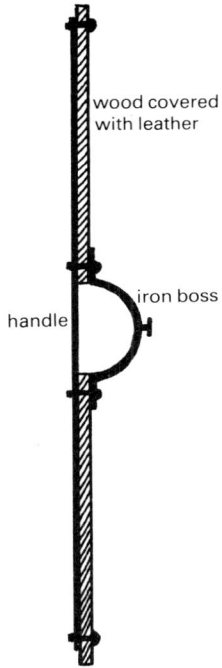

wood covered
with leather

handle

iron boss

This cross-section shows
the construction of a shield.

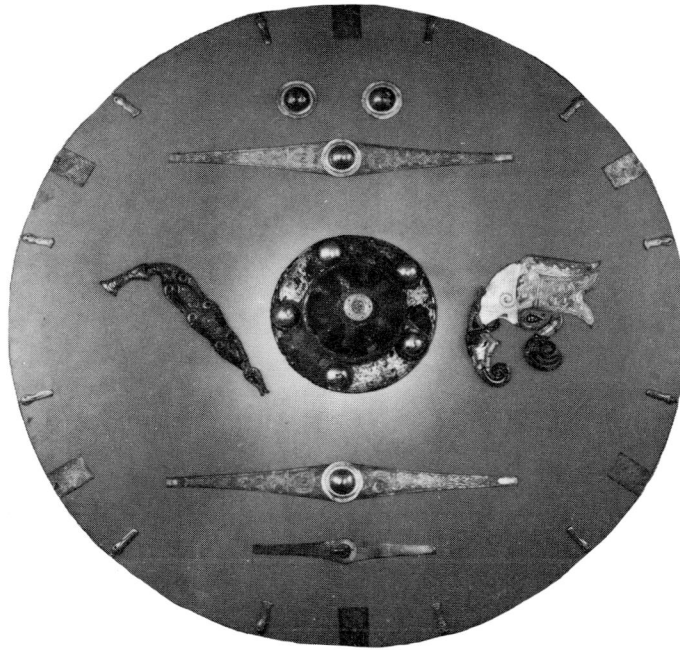

▲

The photograph shows the remains of a shield found at Sutton Hoo. Anglo-Saxon and Viking shields were usually round. This may have been because they were easy to carry when travelling by horseback and were better for hand-to-hand fighting.

Sword from Sutton Hoo burial

Hilt of sword

Swords were only owned by rich and important men. They were very precious and were even given special names. In **Beowulf,** a poem written in the eighth century, the hero's sword is called Naegling. It had been given to Beowulf by his father.

Anglo-Saxon warrior – how do we know he was probably rich and important?

This drawing of a warrior comes from a tenth-century manuscript. He is wearing a chainmail jerkin. Iron rings were linked together or sewn on a leather jerkin. The bottom part was a split skirt, not trousers.

This battle scene comes from a tenth-century manuscript. Not many bows or arrows have been found in excavations, but there are many pictures of them in Anglo-Saxon manuscripts. Why do you think so few have survived? What other weapons can you see in the battle scene?

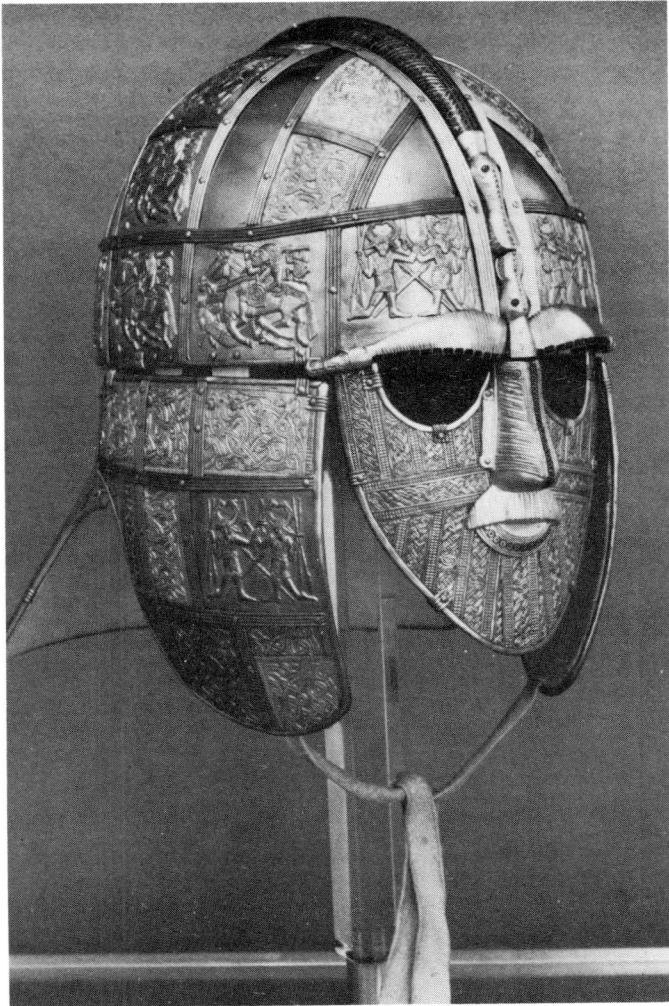

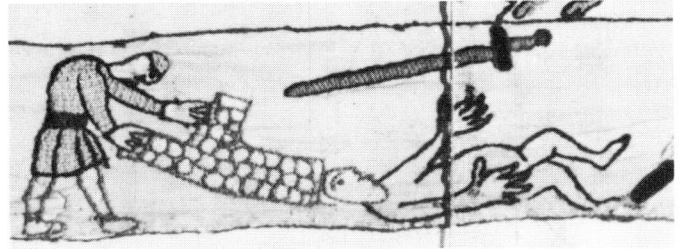

Robbing a dead warrior of his armour – **Bayeux Tapestry**.

This reconstruction of the helmet found at Sutton Hoo shows how archaeologists think it looked when new.
Only the very rich warriors had armour. Like the sword, it was often passed on from father to son.

Above you can see the few pieces of helmet actually found at Sutton Hoo.

An Anglo-Saxon warrior's grave. His iron spear and shield were buried with him. Only the iron boss of the shield has survived. The rest (wood and leather) has rotted.

Defence of the Kingdoms

As the Saxons' settlements grew, they could no longer be protected just by a group of warriors loyal to their lord. A more complicated system of defence became necessary.

Great dykes were built. Nobody is quite certain what these dykes were for but they were probably for defence. It must have taken a great deal of organization and many men to build them.

Devil's Dyke in Cambridgeshire is over 11 km long. Even today the bank is 4 to 5 m high. The ditch is 4 m deep and 20 m wide in some places.

An army also needed to be organized. By AD 800 every village and town had to supply a certain number of men and their weapons for the army. To forget or refuse to turn out when the army was called up was a serious offence and a man could be fined or even lose his land. Desertion from the army was even more serious. A large fine or death could be the penalty.

King Alfred had the idea of dividing the army into two. Whilst one section was on service, the men from the other half could be at home working on their land or at their ordinary jobs. But to call the army out took a long time. Towns had to be defended in case of sudden attack, especially after the Vikings began to raid. Important towns were fortified. Town names with 'bury' in them often come from the Saxon word 'burhs' or fortified place. The people who lived near the burh had to pay for it to be built and supply soldiers to man it. However, often the townspeople did not like paying for these defences and they were not always ready when attacks came.

Aerial view of Wallingford in Berkshire. The outline of the Saxon Burh has been marked in for you.

Houses

end section

(a)

Early Saxon Houses
About AD 400 to AD 600

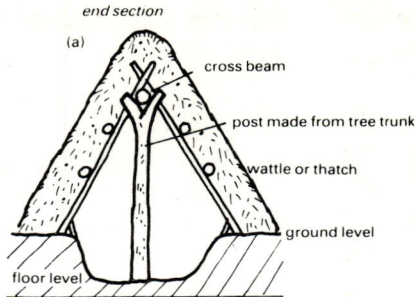

cross beam

post made from tree trunk

wattle or thatch

ground level

floor level

cross section

(c)

small tree trunk
for cross beam

split tree trunks
to make planks

wooden plank across pit to make floor

(b)

approximate size:
4m long 3m wide

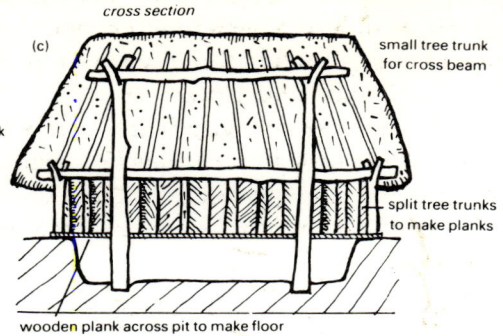

(d)

approximate size: 6m long 5m wide

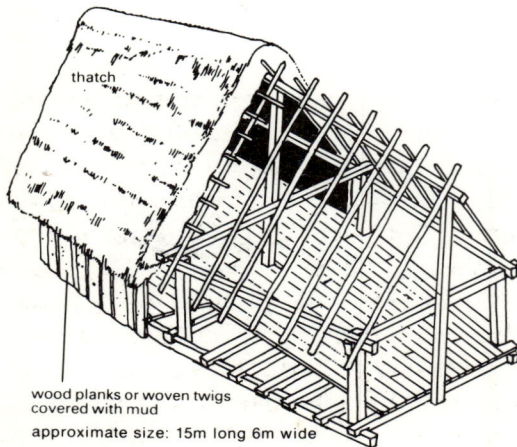

thatch

wood planks or woven twigs
covered with mud

approximate size: 15m long 6m wide

▲
Early Anglo-Saxon houses are called sunken huts because they were built over pits dug out of the ground. Sometimes wooden planks were placed across the top of the pit to form the floor. They had no windows and smoke escaped through the roof which was made of thatch.
Archaeologists are not sure why these huts were built over pits. Can you suggest a reason?

◄ A possible reconstruction of an Anglo-Saxon house at St Neots. Late Anglo-Saxon houses like this one were larger than the earlier ones but were still quite simple. They were often divided into two rooms with a wall made of wattle or woven twigs. Smoke from the fire escaped through a hole in the roof which was thatched or tiled with stone or slate.
Unlike dwellings which date from the twelfth and thirteenth centuries, there is no evidence that the homes of the Anglo-Saxons were shared with the farm animals.

The first Anglo-Saxons to be granted land by the British kings soon chose sites on which to settle, and then sent for their families and friends. Later many more Anglo-Saxons came to Britain and settled.

In the following extract, **Candidus,** a monk who wrote the **Peterborough Chronicle,** tells why Peterborough in Cambridgeshire was chosen as a site. Candidus was writing about a site for a monastery, but it could apply to any settlement.

18. Peterborough was a good spot to build because on one side is fenland, from whch could be obtained logs and kindling for fires, hay for feeding the beasts, thatch for the roofing of houses, fish and waterfowl. On the other side there is pasture and meadows, ploughlands and woodlands. And to the south is the river.

Anglo-Saxon houses shown in the **Bayeux Tapestry.**

The homes of the north German tribes were very different from those of the Romans, as **Tacitus** describes here.

19. It is well known that the German tribes do not live in cities. They live in villages. Even their buildings do not touch each other as ours do, but each one is separate with a clear space around it. Whether they do not know how to build in one continuous line or whether it is a precaution against fire I do not know. They have not learned to use quarry tiles or stones. All building is of timber. They also dig pits in the earth and pile dung in quantitites on the roof to keep out the frost in winter. This also acts as a disguise against their enemies, as they are hard to detect.

What similarities are there between the buildings described by Tacitus and those illustrated on these pages?

Not many Viking houses have been discovered. Those which have been excavated are often similar to Anglo-Saxon ones. At the Viking town of York some two-storey houses have been found. The **Anglo-Saxon Chronicle** tells us that they also had this type of house. But the Vikings did have some new ideas for keeping their houses warm. They probably brought these ideas with them from their cold homelands. In some of the houses excavated at York, the walls were made of two rows of wooden planks and the space in between was filled with twigs – an idea similar to modern 'cavity wall' insulation.

25

Farming and Village Life

Plan of an imaginary Anglo-Saxon village.

As soon as a site was chosen and some kind of shelter built, the settlers had to set about clearing land on which to grow crops and graze animals. At first, settlers probably had their own fields and when these became

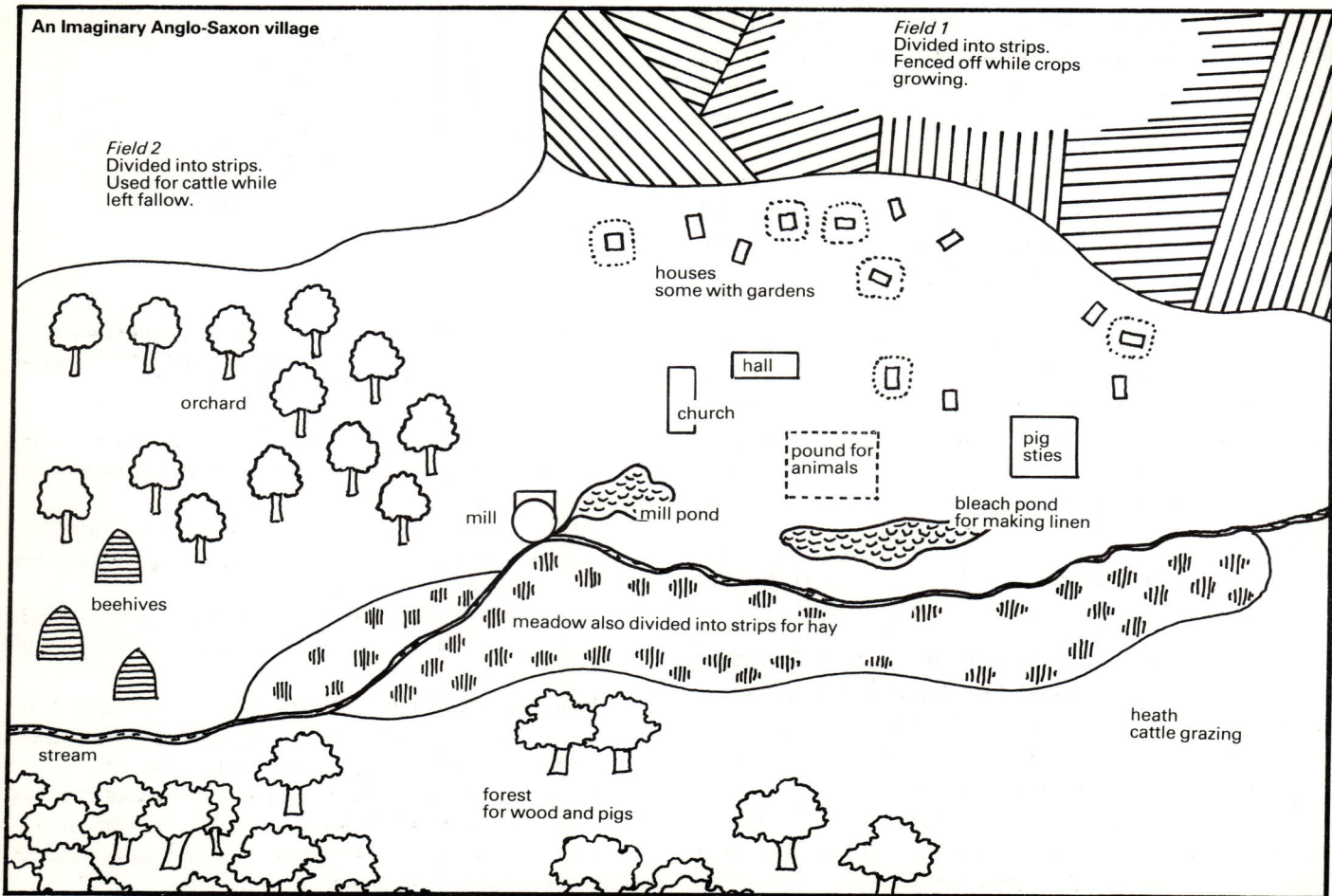

An Imaginary Anglo-Saxon village

Field 1
Divided into strips.
Fenced off while crops growing.

Field 2
Divided into strips.
Used for cattle while left fallow.

houses
some with gardens

orchard

hall

church

pound for animals

pig sties

beehives

mill

mill pond

bleach pond
for making linen

meadow also divided into strips for hay

heath
cattle grazing

stream

forest
for wood and pigs

infertile they would clear more land. Small farms grew.

In some parts of England, the 'open field' or strip system developed. Farms did not consist of small fields divided by hedges. Instead, around the village were two huge fields divided into strips.

Most people in the village had some strips scattered about each field. This meant that everybody had a share of good land and poor land. The number of strips a person had depended on how wealthy he was. He might own his strips or rent them from his lord.

Each year one of the fields would be sown with crops and the other left unsown or fallow. This rested the soil and helped to give it back its goodness. Some of the village animals would graze on the fallow field and so help to manure it.

A person could not make his own decision on what crops he would grow on his strips. Instead, this decision would be made at a meeting of all the strip owners. Different crops would be sown on different parts of the field. A person might also have a garden around his hut on which he could grow vegetables.

What do you think were the disadvantages of having strips in different parts of the field? What might happen if a neighbour was not a good farmer?

The village chief or lord owned much more land than ordinary villagers, and so did the Church. Villagers had to work on this land as well as their own. It was like a tax which they paid in work instead of money. Sometimes villagers had to pay a money tax as well.

Work on the lord's land was organized by his reeve or bailiff. The following extract is from a document called **The Wise Reeve** and describes his work.

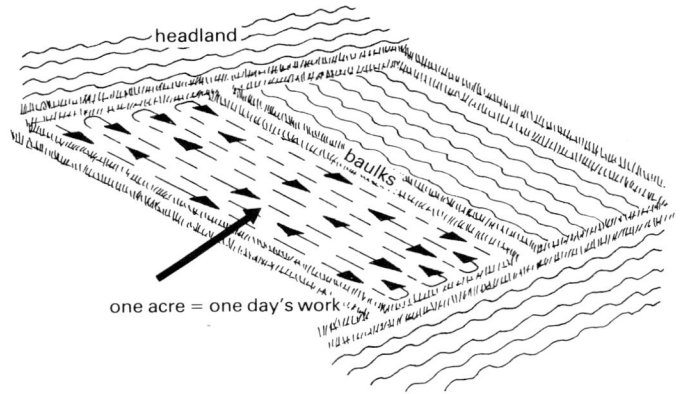

Each strip was roughly one acre in size and separated by a grassy bank or baulk from the next one. This bank could be used as a path to get from one strip to another.

20. In May, June and July: harrowing; carry out manuring; sheep shearing; repairing hedges; attending to the fish weir and mill.
At harvest time: reaping; carrying home and storing the crops, cleaning out the sheep folds and preparing the winter shelters for cattle.
In winter: ploughing; timber to be cut; orchard planted; cattle and pigs attended in the stalls and sties, grain threshed.
In spring: more ploughing; grafting and pruning of fruit trees; planting of vineyards; sowing beans, madder, flax, woad; the garden prepared and many other things.
In spare time: house to be cleaned; tables and benches made; ditches and hedges repaired; tools for miller, shoemaker and carpenter supplied as well as everything else needed for the estate.

January : Ploughing

July : Haymaking

August : Harvesting

December : **Threshing and Winnowing**

These pictures are from the **Anglo-Saxon Calendar.** Using the description of the reeve's work to help you, work out what is being done in each of the pictures. What tools are being used?

This picture of Anglo-Saxon peasants comes from a tenth-century manuscript. Compare their clothes with those of the rich, illustrated on page 32. If you look at the pictures from the **Anglo-Saxon Calendar** opposite, you will notice that even in winter not everybody wore shoes. Most people were probably very poor and life was very hard. Skeletons show that people usually died before the age of 30.

The diagram shows how archaeologists believe the mill
found at Tamworth, Staffs,
worked. The mill was excavated
in 1971 and was probably built
between AD 710 and AD 788.

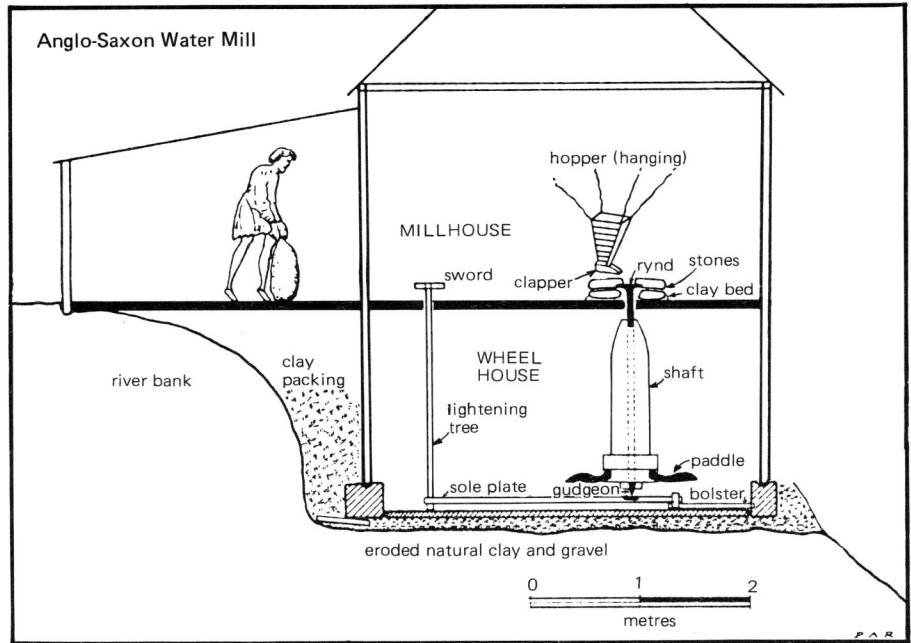

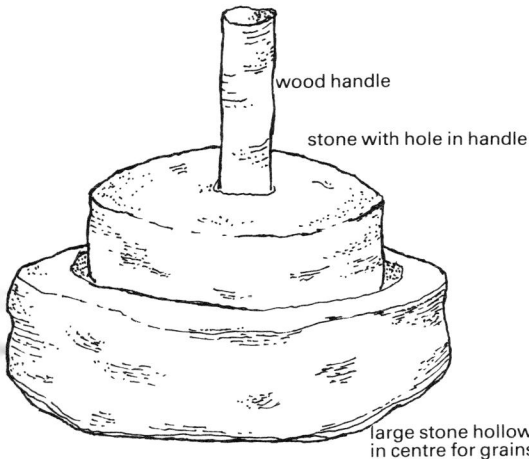

Anglo-Saxon Water Mill

hopper (hanging)

MILLHOUSE

sword   clapper   rynd   stones
                              clay bed

river bank   clay
              packing

WHEEL
HOUSE   shaft

lightening
tree

sole plate   gudgeon   paddle
                          bolster

eroded natural clay and gravel

0   1   2
metres

wood handle

stone with hole in handle

large stone hollowed out
in centre for grains

Querns like this one were used for grinding corn if there was no
mill in the village.

All these cereal crops were used for making bread; barley was
also used for making beer.

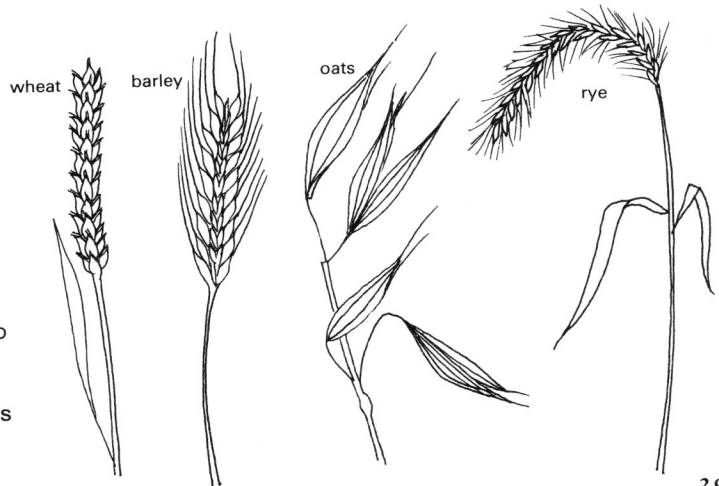

wheat   barley   oats   rye

The women not only had to help the men in the fields; they also had many tasks to perform in the house. What do the following illustrations tell you about these tasks?

These manuscript drawings show women spinning and weaving.

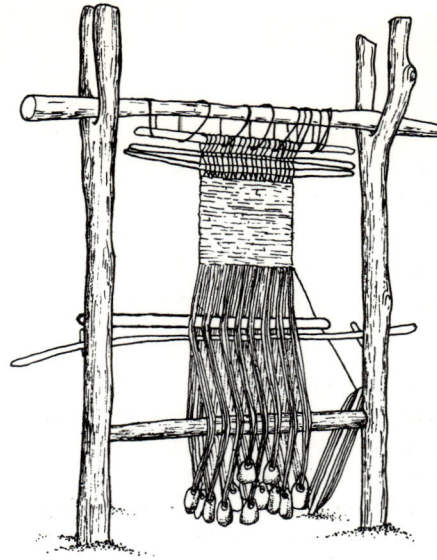

This is a reconstruction of a loom on which wool and flax were woven into cloth. Often bright colour dyes were used. A reddish dye was obtained from madder; blue from woad; bright red from shell-fish; and yellow from saffron crocuses.

On the right you can see some loomweights found at Pakenham.

Sheep were very important for they not only supplied wool and meat, but also milk for butter and cheese. Their skin was valuable for making the parchments on which documents were written.

Cattle, as you can see from the **Anglo-Saxon Calendar,** were used for pulling the farm implements. Only the strongest were kept over winter. The rest were killed and the meat dried and salted. The hides were not only made into shoes, but buckets, door curtains, and many other things. Pigs were also kept. They fed on the woodlands around the village. Deer were eaten, but not rabbits which were introduced to Britain later by the Normans.

Bread was one of the main foods. Potatoes were not introduced to Britain until the sixteenth century. Tea and coffee were unknown, milk could rarely be spared for drinking and the water was probably not very clean, so ale or beer was drunk by most people. Some wine was made in Britain but it was also imported. Mead, a drink made from honey, was drunk by the rich. Honey was also used for sweetening, as sugar had not yet arrived in Britain.

The Lord and the Hall

In some villages the remains of one large building, as well as a number of small huts, have been discovered. Historians believe that these are the remains of the hall, which belonged to the chief or lord of the village.

The following description of a hall is taken from **Beowulf**, a story written in Old English in the eighth century.

21. Tall and wide gabled, the hall towered overhead... Golden tapestries gleamed on the walls and there were many wonderful objects to see... the walls were secured with iron clamps and the door hung on strong iron hinges. The king sat at the banqueting table. Songs were sung and the harp played. The goblet was passed around. At last the benches were cleared away. Pillows and bedding spread on the floor. At their heads the warriors placed their shields and on the benches their helmets, chainmail and spears.

This scene from the **Bayeux Tapestry** shows lords having a banquet. Notice that they are eating only with knives; there are no forks. Here everybody seems to be eating fish. The Anglo-Saxons and Vikings ate a lot of fish once they had become Christians and were not allowed to eat meat on Fridays or during Lent.

This scene from the **Bayeux Tapestry** shows male servants preparing food for a nobleman and his guests. Can you see what food they are preparing?

This picture from the **Anglo-Saxon Calendar** shows a lord hunting with hawks. Other activities of the lord during the times of peace were supervision of the estate and seeing that the law was kept. Sometimes he might tour around the country with the king, or attend a meeting of the witan or king's council.

Shoulder clasps, such as this one found at Sutton Hoo, were used to fasten tunics at the shoulder. They were often inset with jewels or enamel.

The typical clothing of a rich man is shown in these tenth and eleventh-century manuscript drawings. His cloak was fastened with a brooch and often trimmed or lined with fur. On his legs he wore long stockings or hose over which were criss-crossed bandages.

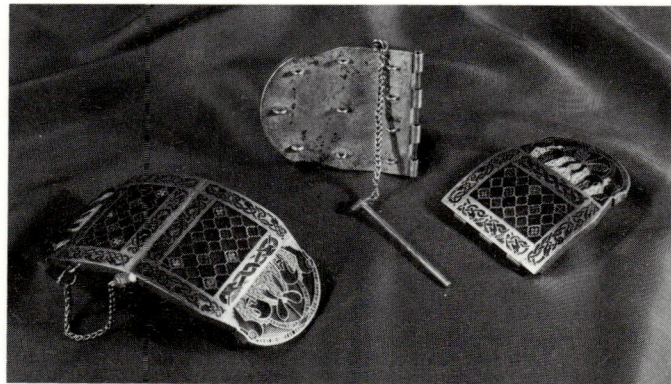

Gold belt buckle found at Sutton Hoo.

The Lord's Lady

A lady sometimes wore, about her waist, a chain or cord holding keys. It indicated her position in society by showing that she had wealth and was important enough to have things that needed guarding.

Compared with later medieval times a Saxon woman was quite well treated. She could own her own property or land: this was not allowed after the Norman Conquest. When she married her husband had to pay a bride price. In early Anglo-Saxon England this went to her father, but later it became the property of the bride.

Although marriages were probably arranged between families, the law clearly stated that, 'No woman shall ever be forced to marry one whom she dislikes, nor sold for money'. If the marriage was unhappy she could obtain a divorce, although when Christianity spread throughout Britain the Church was opposed to divorces.

The typical dress of a rich lady is shown in these tenth and eleventh-century manuscript drawings. Fashion changed a little over the Anglo-Saxon period, but not as much as it does today.

Ninth-century shoe found at York.

33

Kin, Law and Government

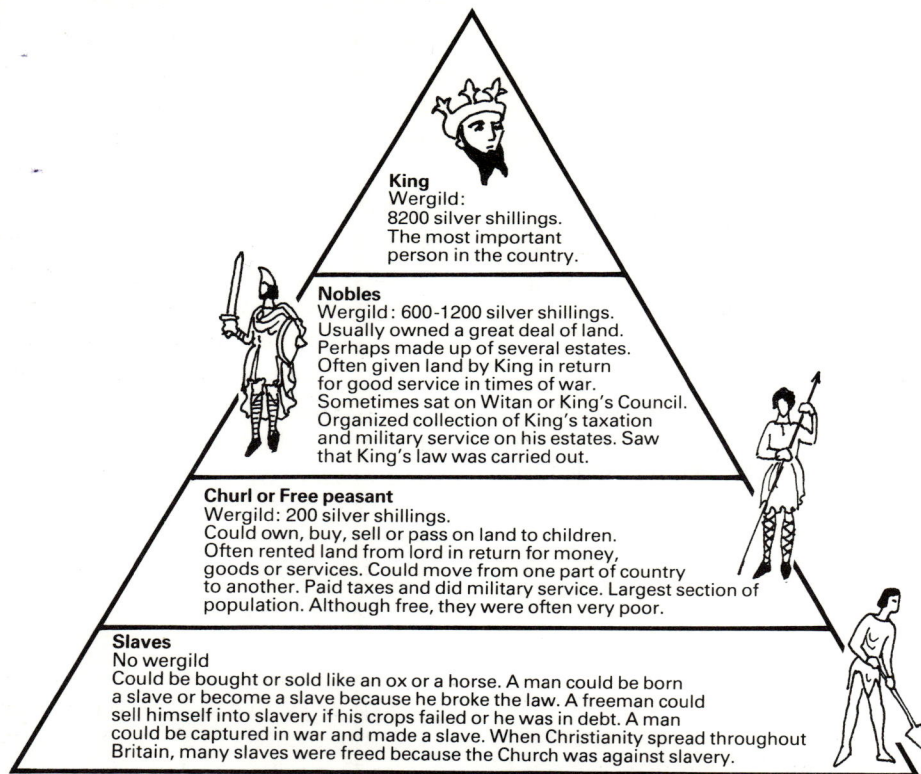

King
Wergild:
8200 silver shillings.
The most important
person in the country.

Nobles
Wergild: 600-1200 silver shillings.
Usually owned a great deal of land.
Perhaps made up of several estates.
Often given land by King in return
for good service in times of war.
Sometimes sat on Witan or King's Council.
Organized collection of King's taxation
and military service on his estates. Saw
that King's law was carried out.

Churl or Free peasant
Wergild: 200 silver shillings.
Could own, buy, sell or pass on land to children.
Often rented land from lord in return for money,
goods or services. Could move from one part of country
to another. Paid taxes and did military service. Largest section of
population. Although free, they were often very poor.

Slaves
No wergild
Could be bought or sold like an ox or a horse. A man could be born
a slave or become a slave because he broke the law. A freeman could
sell himself into slavery if his crops failed or he was in debt. A man
could be captured in war and made a slave. When Christianity spread throughout
Britain, many slaves were freed because the Church was against slavery.

The family – or one's kin – played an important part in Anglo-Saxon and Viking life. It included not only one's father, mother and children, but also one's grandparents, uncles, aunts, cousins and even more distant relations.

A rough guide to the value of wergild.

Wergild
The amount which had to be paid for compensation if a man was killed was called 'wergild'. It was not the same

for everybody: it depended on how important a person was. It also varied at different times and in different kingdoms.

The duties of the family
Here are some of the duties of the family according to laws of seventh- to ninth-century kings.

22. If a husband dies leaving a child, the child should stay with the mother. The father's kinsmen should look after the child's property until he is 10 years old. They should also provide 30 pence a year for the child's upkeep, a cow in summer and an ox in winter.
    If a man is in prison his kin must feed him.
    If a man is captured, his kin should pay his ransom.
    If a man is killed, his kin may revenge his death on the slayer and the slayer's kin. The fee may be settled by compensation or payment to the dead man's family.
    The kin is responsible for bringing wrong-doers to court. If the wrong-doer escapes the kin must pay compensation.

Gradually the kinsman system became less used. The most important loyalty was to one's lord and above him to the king. How would this help the king to govern and to control his kingdom?

Trials
During the early Anglo-Saxon period crimes were tried by 'folk moot', a meeting of villagers or townsfolk. But as the kingdoms grew larger the king needed to be able to control his territory and to impose his own laws. What do **King Alfred's Laws** (set out on page 36) tell you about the ways in which he tried to do this?

The local lord would try cases and by the eleventh century some courts had a kind of jury. If a man was dissatisfied with the verdict of one of the lower courts he could appeal to a higher one, or even to the king.

Trial by ordeal
The support of one's kin was very important to a man accused of a crime. If a man swore on oath that he was not guilty and could persuade his kin to believe him and also to swear that he was not guilty, he had a good chance of going free. However, it was a very serious offence to swear an oath which you knew was not true. If your kin would not support you, you could try to prove your innocence by Ordeal or the 'Judgement of God'. In the Ordeal, God would accept the innocent but reject the guilty.

The following description of ordeals is taken from **King Athelstan's Laws** AD 924.

23. *By cold water*: a man must be bound with rope and he must be thrown into the water. If he is innocent he will sink one and a half ells (1.7 m). If he is guilty, he will float, for God will reject him.
    By hot water: to take place in the church building. For those who have committed a serious crime, the arm must be plunged into a cauldron of boiling water up to the elbow; for less serious crimes plunged to the wrist. A stone must be taken out of the cauldron and carried nine feet (2.7 m). The hand must be then wrapped. If found to be clean and not festering after three days the man is innocent.

Punishments

Those who were guilty were punished. **King Alfred's Laws,** AD 871, included the following list of punishments.

24. 1. Everyman's oath should be true and his promises kept.
    2. If a man breaks his pledges or oaths, he must spend 40 days in prison.
    3. If anyone plots against the king's life, or shelters the king's enemies, he is liable to lose his life and all that he owns.
    4. If a man steals in church his hand is to be cut off or he may pay a fine in proportion to his blood money or wergild.
    5. If a man says false things in public against another, he is to have his tongue cut out or pay a fine in proportions to his blood money.
    6. A man may fight on behalf of his kinsman, but he may not fight against his own lord. That we do not allow.

Everyone should be fairly tried, with one judgement for the rich and poor, for those dear to you and those you hate.

Anglo-Saxon manuscript showing people being punished. What is happening to them?

King and his advisers. They formed a council called a witan.

The organization of the kingdom in the eleventh century.

Person	Territory	Court and Duties
King	Kingdom	Witan – Council of advisers and Court of Justice
Shire Reeve (Sheriff)	Shire	Shire Moot – Law Court – held twice a year Organization of army and defence Collection of taxes Carrying out King's commands
Hundredman or Thane	Hundred or Wapentake or Riding	Law Court with 12 jury or doomsmen Collection of taxes Carrying out King's commands
Reeve	Folk Moot	Village matters, distribution of field strips, straying cattle, etc.

Town Life

When the Anglo-Saxons first invaded Britain they were farmers and mainly settled in the countryside. As a result many of the Roman cities became deserted. An Old English poem describes one:

25. . . . The city buildings crumble, the bold works of the giants decay. Roofs have fallen in, towers collapsed, The ruins have tumbled to the plain. . . .

Gradually farming improved and the villagers grew more food than they needed. They began to exchange their surplus food for different goods from the other villages. One village would become a centre of trade for the surrounding area. Craftsmen, blacksmiths, potters and weavers would also gather there to sell their goods on market days. The village developed into a town.

At first, goods were exchanged for other things which people needed, but as trade grew this became too awkward a method of trading. Coins were introduced and many towns were granted the right by the kings to mint (make) coins. Coins were also needed by the English to pay the Danegeld. So much English money went to the Danes that more Saxon coins are found in Scandinavia than in Britain.

A silver penny from the reign of King Ethelred of Wessex.

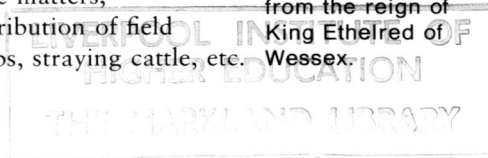

This panel from the Franks casket shows a blacksmith and his tools. The casket was made in about AD 700 of whale bone and was carved with pictures of different scenes.

Towns had special laws and rights granted by the king. They were not ruled by a lord as were most villages. Instead the most important man in the town was the king's reeve. He collected the taxes, saw that the law was carried out and granted licences.

The craftsmen in the town often joined together into 'guilds'. These were groups of men from one craft who made sure that standards of workmanship were being kept up and that apprentices were trained properly.

Other towns grew up around the large monasteries. Later, when the kingdoms became more powerful, each king needed a centre from which to organize the collection of taxes and the administration of his laws. So towns became more important.

When the Viking raids began, these important centres had to be defended. Walls were built and even more craftsmen and traders moved to the safety of the town. When the Vikings settled in Britain, they too developed towns to administer their kingdom and to be centres of trade.

By 1066 about ten per cent of the population lived in towns, more than in any other country in Europe. Historians have worked out the population of some towns in 1066. You will see from the following list that most towns were no bigger than a village is today.

London	12 000 people
York	8 000
Lincoln	5 000
Norwich	5 000
Thetford	4 000
Oxford	3 500
Colchester	2 000

Towns which were also ports must have been particularly busy. They increased their wealth by levying (charging) tolls.

Tolls charged at Billingsgate, London, in the tenth century.

Small ship	half penny
Larger ship with sails	one penny
Merchantman	four pence
Ship with cargo of planks	one plank
Small ship with cargo of fish	one half penny
Large ship with cargo of fish	one penny
Ship from Rouen France with wine or blubberfish	30 pence and 5 percent of the fish to be given
Hampers of hens	one hen
Hampers of eggs	five eggs per hamper
Women with dairy produce (butter and cheese)	one penny a fortnight.

A coin die found at York.

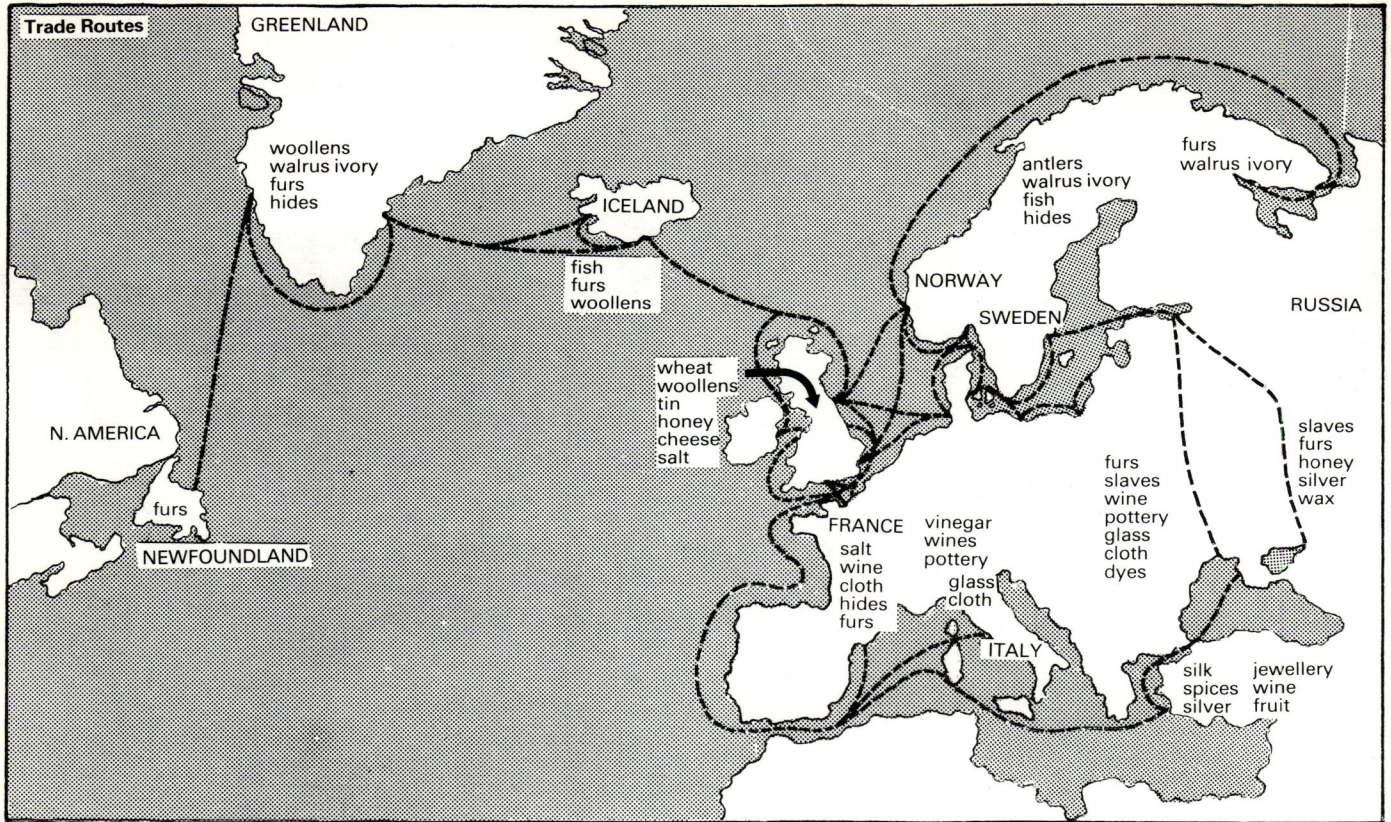

Trade Routes

GREENLAND

woollens
walrus ivory
furs
hides

ICELAND

fish
furs
woollens

NORWAY

SWEDEN

RUSSIA

antlers
walrus ivory
fish
hides

furs
walrus ivory

N. AMERICA

furs

NEWFOUNDLAND

wheat
woollens
tin
honey
cheese
salt

FRANCE

salt
wine
cloth
hides
furs

vinegar
wines
pottery

glass
cloth

furs
slaves
wine
pottery
glass
cloth
dyes

slaves
furs
honey
silver
wax

ITALY

silk
spices
silver

jewellery
wine
fruit

Trade routes showing where goods came from.

You can see from the map that ships came to Britain
from many different places, with many different cargoes.
They exchanged their cargoes for British products to
trade abroad.

Religion

When the Anglo-Saxons and the Vikings came to Britain, they did not worship the Christian God, but many different gods. Evidence of these gods comes from many sources: the days of the week, for example, are named after Anglo-Saxon or Viking gods.

Tuesday	Tiw, Tyr: the god of war or battles.
Wednesday	Woden, Odin, Othin: the king of the gods, god of the dead; also known as Grim.
Thursday	Thor, Thunor: god of thunder and lightning. His symbol was a hammer.
Friday	Frigg, Freyja: wife of Woden and goddess of fertility.

As the Anglo-Saxons and Vikings did not write, we know very little about how these gods were worshipped. Place names sometimes suggest where they were worshipped. Here are just a few. See if there are any in your district.

Wednesbury, Wednesfield, Wensley, Wansdyke	Woden
Tuesley, Tysley, Tysoe	Tiw
Thursley, Thurstable, Thunderfield, Thundersley	Thor
Harrow, Harrowden	Hearg or temple

Cremation urn and grave goods. After the Anglo-Saxons and Vikings became Christians, they stopped cremating bodies and burying goods with them.

Christianity

The following extract is from **Beowulf,** a poem written when the Anglo-Saxons had been converted to Christianity. The author, however, knew the folk tales of his ancestors.

26. Then the lords began to build a burial mound... it was high and broad and could be seen far out at sea. It took them 10 days to finish their monument to their hero. It had a wall of earth around it... and inside the mound they put rings and jewels and ornaments. All his gold and treasure, they were left there too—and there they still remain to this very day...
Finally they rode round his grave mound... mourning his death, praising his death, praising his greatness and all his brave deeds.

The Britons had been converted to Christianity during Roman times. Although the Anglo-Saxons drove out the Christians and destroyed heir churches over much of Britain, Christianity was not completely dead. Some Britons, the Welsh and the people of eastern Ireland remained Christians and where they survived so did the Christian religion.

About AD 563 some monks from Ireland, led by a man named Columba, settled on a small island called Iona off the coast of Scotland. From there they moved on to the Scottish mainland and began the work of converting the heathen Scots to Christianity. Not long after this the

This photograph is of the burial mound at Sutton Hoo. There are several other photographs in this book which show objects found in the mound by the estuary of the River Deben, Suffolk.

Pope in Rome decided to send missionaries to the Anglo-Saxon part of Britain.

The following two extracts are from **Bede's History of the English Church and People**, AD 597.

27. Pope Gregory sent Augustine and 40 monks to Britain. The most powerful king at this time was Ethelbert of Kent, whose wife Bertha was already a Christian because she was a Frank (French). The king met the missionaries and told them, 'Your words and promises are good, but they are new and I do not know whether to believe them. I cannot just abandon my old beliefs. But as you have travelled a long way to tell us about what you believe is true, I will not harm you and I will give you permission to preach and win anybody you can to your religion.

Why do you think Augustine chose to start his work in Britain with Ethelbert's Kingdom?

28. As soon as the missionaries settled in Canterbury they began to preach. They would not accept a lot of costly gifts, but lived very simply and only accepted the necessities of life. Before long a number of the heathens, admiring the simplicity of their holy lives and liking what they heard about the Christian God, were baptized. Later the King himself was converted.

While St Augustine's monks were working and converting people to Christianity in the south of England, another group of monks left the Scottish island of Iona and set up a monastery at Lindisfarne off the coast of Northumbria.

Unification of the Church
Despite the work of Augustine, Columba and Aidan of

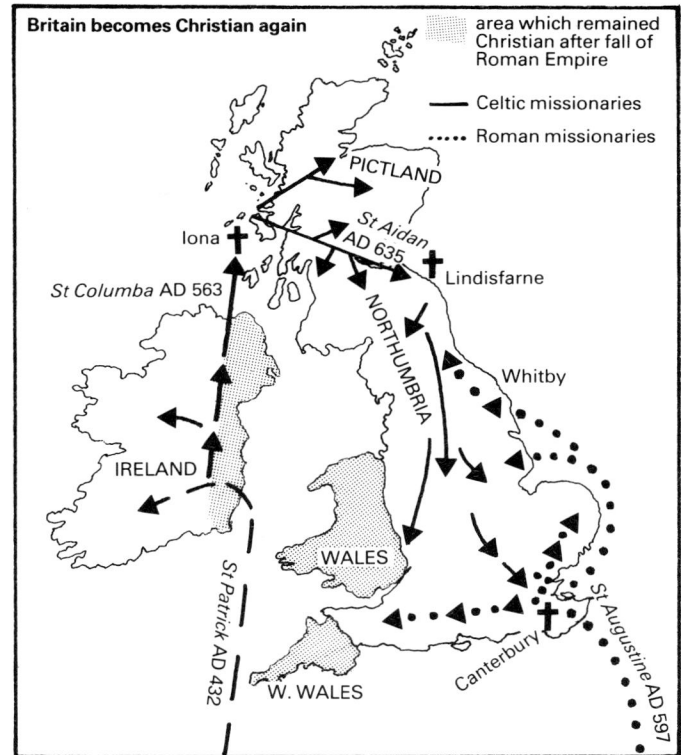

Britain becomes Christian again.

Lindisfarne it was many years before all Britain became Christian.

The spread of Christianity was not helped by the division within the Church itself. The monks who originally came from Scotland and Ireland had, after the fall of the Roman Empire, been cut off from the headquarters of the Church in Rome. The way the Scottish or Celtic Church worshipped God had begun to

This cross, from a Christian grave at Middleton, has carvings which show a heathen burial with grave goods.

vary from the Roman way. The two Churches had obvious differences: for example they celebrated Easter on different days. Such differences led to arguments and made the work of the missionaries more difficult.

One Northumbrian king, Oswiu, was a Celtic Christian. His wife was a Roman Christian. Oswiu realized it would be much better if the Churches could settle their differences. He called a conference or Synod at Whitby in AD 664.

After the Synod it was agreed that the English Churches should all follow the ways of Rome. Bishops and monks could now travel from one English kingdom to another bringing all the Churches into one organization. This gave the kingdoms a great sense of unity and helped to lessen the differences between them. As the kingdoms gradually joined together, the kingdom of England and the Church territory of England became the same.

The Celtic Church remained strong in Wales and Scotland for a further 100 years, but by the ninth century it too had accepted the Pope in Rome as head of the Christian Church.

Messengers constantly travelled to and from Rome bringing with them new ideas. Christianity was the religion of most of Europe, so now Britain was no longer separated from mainland Europe by different beliefs, but was part of Europe or Christendom.

The Vikings and the Christians

As we learn from the **Anglo-Saxon Chronicle,** even after the Christians in Britain had settled their differences, their troubles were not over.

29. AD 794: For beginning with Northumbria the heathens burned all the monasteries, going throughout all England killing all the monks and nuns, taking care that none should live to tell of the massacres and warn others to be on their guard.

The heathens were of course the Vikings, or Danes as they were often called.

Very few Viking burials are found in Britain. Perhaps the following extracts from the **Anglo-Saxon Chronicle** and **Egils Saga** explain why.

30. AD 878: Alfred fought against the heathens and defeated them. They left hostages and promised to leave the kingdom. In addition they promised to be baptized. Three weeks later they kept their promise and were baptized. King Alfred was Godfather to the Danish King.

It was a common custom amongst those Viking merchants and warriors who settled in England to be baptized. Men who were baptized had full contact with the Christians. But they kept their own faith as well so they could use whatever faith they wished.

The Church and Learning
The leaders of the Church often acted as advisers to the kings. They helped them to administer their kingdoms and Church teaching influenced the laws of the kingdoms.

Christianity is a religion based on the teachings written in the Bible. As Christianity spread, monasteries were built where monks and nuns could lead simple lives praying to God. The monasteries started schools to teach the monks and nuns to read the Holy Books and to copy them out for other people to use.

The monks spent many hours decorating or 'illuminating' the bibles and other holy books which they wrote, to make them special and beautiful for God. Sometimes they decorated the capital letters beginning each page.
This is a page from the Lindisfarne Gospel which was written in Latin, the language used by the Church all over Europe. Sometimes books were written in English. King Alfred ordered books to be written in English so that ordinary people could read them.

f	u	th	a	r	k
g	w	h	n	i	j
p	e	R	s	t	b
ee	m	l	ng	d	o

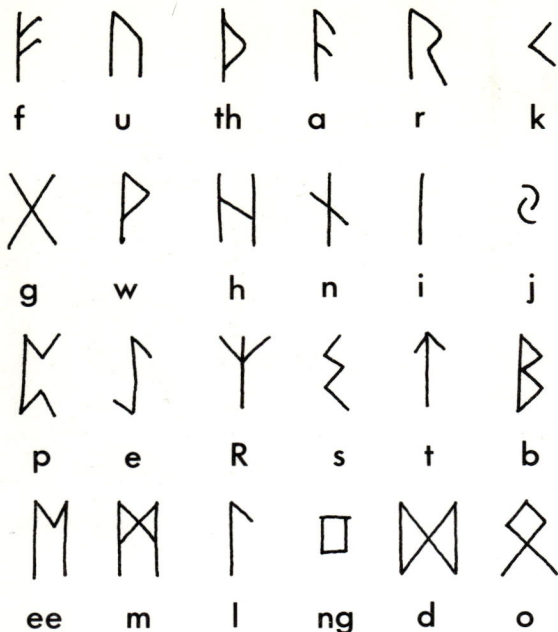

The Anglo-Saxons and Vikings had some writing, but they did not use it as much as the Christians used theirs. Our only evidence of this writing is in the form of inscriptions known as runes. The letters consisted of straight lines, thus making it easier to carve them out of stone. On the photograph of the Franks Casket on page 38 you will see some runes.

The monasteries often also had schools where nobles could send their children to learn to read and write. People began to realize how useful it was to be able to write things down. Messages could be sent long distances without the meaning getting changed. Records could be kept of what happened or who owned land, taxes could be collected more efficiently. Kings had their laws written down so that people could know exactly what they were.

Church Buildings

As **Bede** tells us, the first churches were those restored from the ruins of Roman churches. But as Christianity spread to new villages more churches had to be built.

Curved arch.

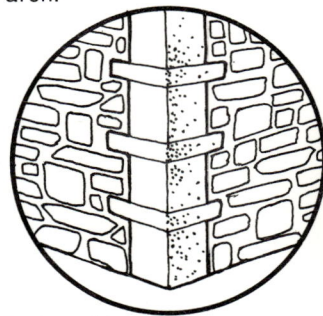

'Long and short work'.

Many of our churches have some Anglo-Saxon work in them. You can often tell if a church was started in Anglo-Saxon times by how it was built. See if your local church has any Anglo-Saxon parts.

Barnack Church in Cambridgeshire has an Anglo-Saxon tower (the top was added later). Notice the rounded archways, the carving and the 'long and short work' on the corners.

Like this church at Greensted in Essex, some churches were built of wood.

Like this church at Escomb, many Anglo-Saxon churches were built of stone.

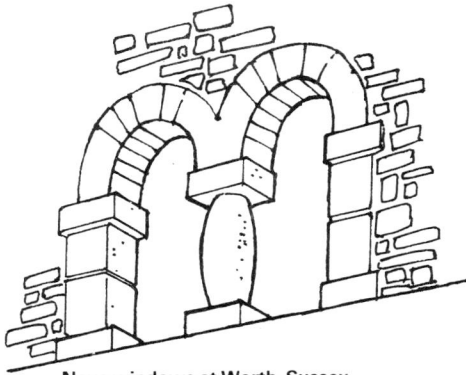

Nave windows at Worth, Sussex

Anglo-Saxon windows like these were usually quite small and did not contain glass. Can you suggest why?

St Martin's, Canterbury – built on the site of a Roman church. ▶

The Anglo-Saxon Period and Us

The Britain of the Anglo-Saxons and Vikings was a very different place from the country we know today. Using figures in the **Domesday Book,** written for the Normans in AD 1086, it has been estimated that the population of England was about one and a quarter million. The population of Wales and Scotland would have been much smaller.

Many parts of Britain were still thickly forested or covered with natural heathland. Marshes and fens were undrained. Eagles and cranes were common. Hawkley and Cranford are places named after birds rarely seen today. Wolves and bears still lived in the forests. These animals gave their names to Beverley, Barford and Woolpit (a pit for trapping wolves). Travel was still difficult; water transport was often the best. According to the **Peterborough Chronicle:**

31. Ramsey, Thorney and Crowland cannot be travelled to except by boat. Ely is surrounded on all sides by fen and water. This fen extends for sixty miles.

Most ordinary people were unable to read or write and spent the whole of their lives in the village in which they were born. That village provided everything they needed.

After Christianity spread across Britain, the Church played an important part in life. Important events in people's lives were marked by church services. Holiday were the holy festivals like Easter and Christmas. The most terrible fate that could befall a person was to be cut off from the Church as a whole and thus lose all hope of going to heaven after death.

Many children did not live to adulthood and, even if they did survive, lack of medical knowledge meant that many illnesses or injuries could not be treated and caused early death.

In some ways, however, life was similar to today. People had to obey the laws and pay taxes. The king or government was expected to protect the kingdom in times of trouble, to pass new laws when they were needed and see that they were carried out.

Reminders of the Anglo-Saxons and Vikings can still be found in our everyday lives. They established many of the villages still lived in today and set the boundaries of parishes and the old counties of England. Finally, the English language owes much to their influence: many of the most common English words are taken from their languages.

Some Anglo-Saxon and Viking words. There are many more.

England, call, eggs, little, Kingdom, window, penny, leaves, law, sky, stood, green, gate, anger, fall, yellow, son, low, road, earth, husband, loose, often, dust, sister, ugly, hard, cold, he, wrong, heart, morning, man, happy, hand, life, hill, bread, more, light, take.

Do you think you would be able to hold a conversation without using Saxon or Viking words? Anyone with the surname Webster, Smith, Edwards, Cook, Browning, or one ending in 'son' uses Anglo-Saxon or Viking all the time, especially if they live in a 'ton', 'ing', 'by', or a 'thorpe'.